Take a trip to
WEST
GERMANY

Text and photographs by
Chris Fairclough

General Editor
Henry Pluckrose

Franklin Watts
London   New York   Sydney   Toronto

35415

Words about West Germany

Alps
Autobahn

Bavaria
beer
Ludwig van
    Beethoven
East Berlin
West Berlin
Bierfest
Bonn
Bundeshaus

chemicals
clocks
coal
Cologne (Köln)

Danke
Deutschmark
Dom
Dortmund

Elbe
electrical goods
Essen

flower market
Frankfurt
frankfurters

Hamburg

iron

Moselle
Munich
    (München)

Pfennig

Rhine
Ruhr

steel

trams

vineyards
Volkswagen

wheat

Franklin Watts Limited
8 Cork Street
London W1

ISBN UK edition: 0 85166 927 1
ISBN US edition: 0 531 04320 7
Library of Congress Catalog Card No:
81–50032

© Franklin Watts Limited 1981

Printed in Great Britain by
E. T. Heron, Essex and London.

Maps by Brian and Constance Dear, and
Tony Payne.
Design by Tim Healey.
The author and publisher would like to
thank the following for kind permission to
reproduce photographs: Goethe Institute,
London (cover, 12, 13, 14, 17, 19, 24, 28);
Ian Goodwin (3); The Crafts Council of
Great Britain (18); Stephen Emmerson
(31); Frieder Blickle (11).
The author will also like to thank C.D.G.

West Germany is a large country in the middle of Europe. It stretches from the mountainous Alps in the south to flat coastlands in the north. There are many thriving industrial cities and small villages too, set in beautiful countryside.

West Germany was formed after World War II, when the old Germany was divided into two new countries: East Germany and West Germany. Bonn is the capital of West Germany. The West German parliament is called the Bundeshaus.

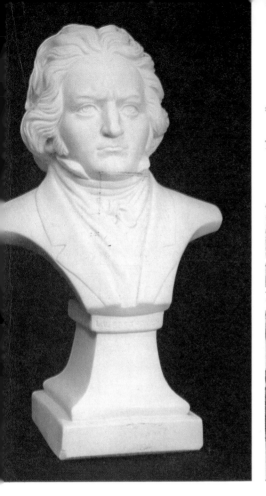

The German people are famous for their love of music. One of the world's greatest composers, Ludwig van Beethoven, was born in Bonn. His house still stands in the old part of the city.

5

This shows West German stamps
and money. There are 100 Pfennigs
in each Deutschmark.

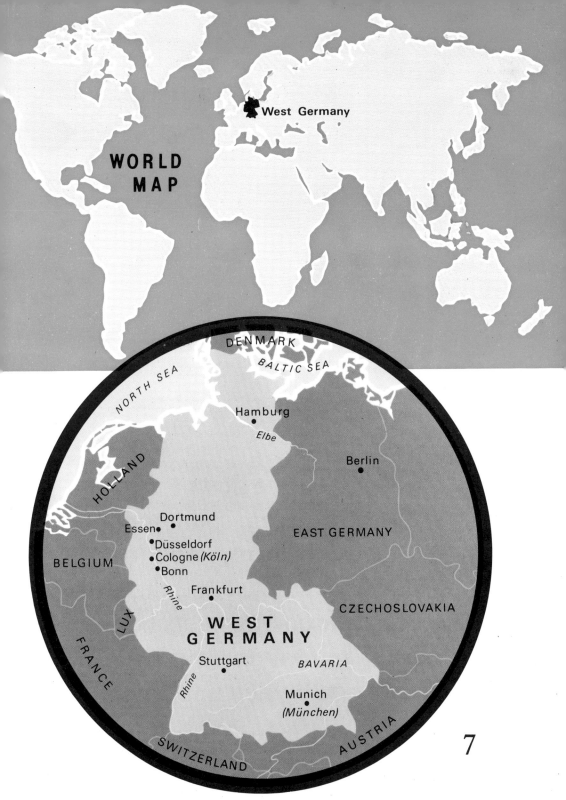

WORLD
MAP

West Germany

DENMARK

BALTIC SEA

NORTH SEA

Hamburg

Elbe

Berlin

HOLLAND

Dortmund

Essen

Düsseldorf

EAST GERMANY

Cologne (Köln)

Bonn

BELGIUM

Frankfurt

Rhine

CZECHOSLOVAKIA

LUX

WEST
GERMANY

FRANCE

Stuttgart

BAVARIA

Rhine

Munich
(München)

SWITZERLAND

AUSTRIA

7

The River Rhine flows through West Germany from south to north. It has always been an important link between regions, and there are many historic castles on its banks. Some of the finest were built over 200 years ago by rich noblemen.

The Rhine is still a major
transport link. Barges and larger
vessels carry goods between West
Germany's inland cities and the
mouth of the river in Holland on the
North Sea.

Cologne is a beautiful city on the Rhine. Its German name is Köln. The cathedral is over 700 years old, and is one of the largest in Europe. It is called the Dom, and its spires are nearly 160 m. (525 ft) high.

Artists draw pictures with chalk on the pavements near Cologne Cathedral. Here, the artist has copied a work by a great painter. Tourists give him money. The artist has written "Danke" (thank you).

North of Cologne lie the industrial regions of Dortmund and Essen in the rich coalfields which are in the river Ruhr district. The coal is used for smelting iron and steel at many great works nearby.

West German industries are very efficient. The people have a reputation for hard work. Cars are a major export. Motor companies such as Volkswagen, Opel and Mercedes export cars and vans to almost every country in the world.

The northern region of West Germany contains much flat farming land. The farmers raise dairy cattle, and grow cereal crops such as wheat, rye, barley and oats. Here you can see a combine harvester at work.

West German exports, such as
cars, electrical goods and chemicals
are shipped all over the world.
Hamburg is at the mouth of the
River Elbe on the North Sea coast.
It is one of the biggest and busiest
ports in Europe.

The southern part of West
Germany rises towards the Alps, the
great mountain range in the heart of
Europe. The southern region is
called Bavaria. In winter, the
mountains are covered with snow.

16

Munich is the largest city in Bavaria. It is called München in German. The city is famous for brewing beer. There are Bierfests (beer festivals) every year. Visitors come to sample the various types of beer.

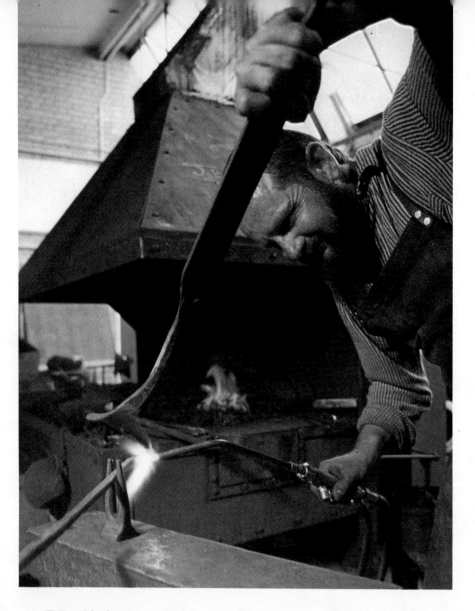

Holidaymakers flock to Bavaria.
The tourists buy local handicrafts.
Bavaria is famous for its ironwork.

The West Germans are keen sports fans. Football is one of the most popular sports. The Olympic Games were held in Munich in 1972. This stadium was built specially for the Games. It holds 80,000 people.

Flower markets are a common sight in many West German towns. The stall holders arrive early in the morning. They hope to sell their flowers before it gets too hot and the flowers start to wilt.

People use trams to get about in many cities. The trams run on a fixed track and stop at stations in the street. Some streets are completely closed to traffic, making shopping easier and more enjoyable.

Most West German city-dwellers
live in flats. Many modern blocks,
like this one in Cologne, are built on
the edge of the city, and are
surrounded by parks.

22

Flats usually have large windows and balconies. Furniture is generally modern and very carefully chosen. Indoor plants are very popular and some flats have balcony gardens.

On their first day at school, children take cones filled with sweets and presents from their parents. The primary school is called a "Grundschule" (ground school).

West German children only go to primary school in the mornings. They begin their lessons at 8.30 and finish at 1.30. However all pupils are expected to do homework in the afternoon. They carry their books in large satchels.

West Germany borders nine other countries. Some children grow up speaking two languages: For example, children living near the French border may speak French as well as German. English is the main foreign language taught in schools.

West Germans are fond of good food. Sausages, called Würst, are particularly liked. There are over one hundred types. Some are named according to region. For example, frankfurters come from Frankfurt.

Most West German wines are white. The grapes are grown especially in vineyards in the valleys of the Rhine and the Moselle rivers. Local villagers hold annual festivals to celebrate the grape harvest.

West Germany is a large country
so it needs good communications.
Most of the railways are electric.
Inter-city trains can travel at 200 km
(144 miles) per hour.

West Germany's roads are fast and modern. Motorways are called Autobahns. Some of them hold ten lanes of traffic. A network of Autobahns covers the country and you can go right across West Germany on them.

   Before World War II, Berlin was
the capital of Germany. Today,
Berlin is inside East Germany.
However, the city is divided. East
Berlin is part of East Germany, but
West Berlin belongs to West
Germany. A wall separates them.

Index